Count the dragons, knights, castles & crowns!

The Dragon Counting Book
For Children Aged 2 - 5!

D1309124

Brought to you by the authors of....
'Count The Aliens, Spaceships, Stars & Planets'

GOOD LUCK...

HOW MANY CASTLES ARE THERE?

THERE ARE **THREE** CASTLES ...

1

2

3

Which castle would you live in?

HOW MANY GREEN DRAGONS

 CAN YOU FIND HERE?

THERE ARE **FIVE** GREEN DRAGONS!

1

2

3

4

5

How many did you count?

HOW MANY CROWNS ARE THERE?

THERE IS JUST **ONE** CROWN!

Kings and Queens both wear crowns!

ARE THERE MORE GREEN DRAGONS OR RED DRAGONS?

THERE ARE **SEVEN** RED DRAGONS AND **FOUR** GREEN DRAGONS...

SO THERE ARE **MORE RED DRAGONS** THAN GREEN DRAGONS!

HOW MANY BLUE DRAGONS

 ## CAN YOU FIND HERE?

THERE ARE **FOUR** BLUE DRAGONS!

1   2   3   4

4

HOW MANY OF THE DRAGONS HAVE YELLOW SPOTS?

TWO OF THE DRAGONS HAVE YELLOW SPOTS!

1 2

HOW MANY OF THE DRAGONS ARE SLEEPING?

ONLY **ONE** OF THE DRAGONS IS ASLEEP... (SHHH)

1

ARE THERE MORE SWORDS OR MORE GOLD NECKLACES?

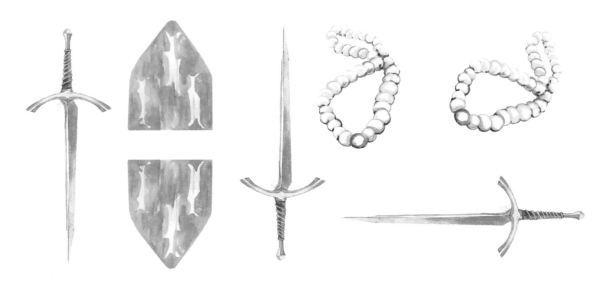

THERE ARE **FOUR** GOLD NECKLACES AND **THREE** SWORDS...

SO THERE ARE **MORE** NECKLACES THAN SWORDS!

HOW MANY CAVES CAN YOU COUNT?

THERE ARE **SEVEN** CAVES!

1   2   3   4   5   6   7

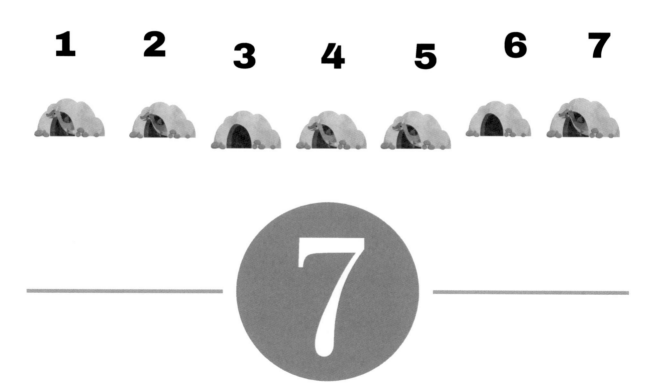

7

HOW MANY ORANGE DRAGONS CAN YOU COUNT?

THERE ARE **TWO** ORANGE DRAGONS...

1

2

Did you count correctly?

HOW MANY KNIGHTS CAN YOU COUNT?

THERE ARE **THREE** KNIGHTS!

1   2   3

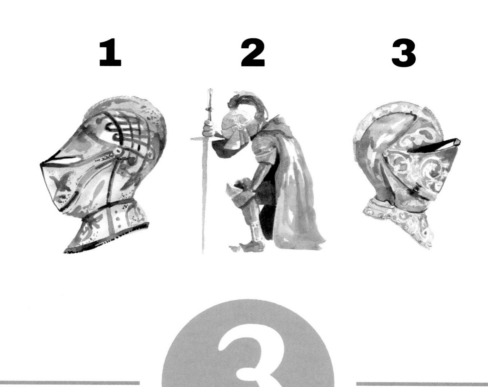

3

ARE THERE MORE BLUE DRAGONS OR MORE RED SHIELDS?

THERE ARE **EIGHT** RED SHIELDS AND **FOUR** BLUE DRAGONS...

SO THERE ARE **MORE RED SHIELDS** THAN BLUE DRAGONS!

ARE THERE MORE CASTLES OR MORE COINS?

THERE ARE **FOUR** CASTLES, AND TWO COINS...

SO THERE ARE **MORE CASTLES** THAN THERE ARE COINS!

HOW MANY OF THE CAVES
HAVE DRAGONS INSIDE THEM?

1

THERE ARE THREE CAVES
THAT HAVE DRAGONS INSIDE THEM!

2

3

Are you ready for the final question?

HOW MANY TIMES CAN YOU
COUNT THIS DRAGON
IN THE WHOLE BOOK?

(INCLUDING THE ONE ON THIS PAGE & ANY
YOU SEE ON THE ANSWER PAGES...)

THE ANSWER IS . . .

13

WE HOPE YOU AND YOUR CHILDREN ENJOYED LEARNING FROM THIS DRAGON COUNTING BOOK..

WE HAVE A WHOLE RANGE OF COUNTING BOOKS AVAILABLE ON AMAZON – JUST SEARCH *'PRINCE JAMES PRESS'*

Made in the USA
Monee, IL
25 May 2020